LET YOUR STORIES GUIDE YOU

A COMPASS
for the
HEART

*A 90-day journal
for self-reflection*

BERNADETTE JIWA

Published in Australia by Perceptive Press.
www.thestoryoftelling.com

DISCLAIMER

National Library of Australia Publication Data
available via www.nla.gov.au

ISBN: 978-0-9944328-5-8

Printed in the United States of America

Cover & Interior Design: Swish Design

First Edition

One sees clearly only with the heart. Anything essential is invisible to the eyes.

—ANTOINE DE SAINT-EXUPÉRY

*Stories are data
that teach us
emotional truths.*

INTRODUCTION

Once upon a time. The four words that begin our earliest childhood lessons. Long before we know how to tell stories, we understand that they are our teachers. We are transported to worlds where heroes and heroines find themselves in circumstances, faced with choices, that cause them to change. By listening to these stories, we learn ways that we too might be braver, more courageous and true to ourselves.

We are the hero or heroine of our stories. The character, in circumstances, facing choices we must navigate. How we navigate those circumstances, make those choices and the outcomes we experience as a result, teaches us something about trusting ourselves to do the right thing. Every day, there's an opportunity for us to use yesterday's stories as wise counsel for tomorrow. That's what this journal is about—gathering everyday life lessons for your future self and understanding how to call on yourself in good times and in bad.

Wisdom is not bestowed—it is earned.

This journal will help you to record your stories and reflect on how they made you stronger—more courageous and creative, insightful and intuitive, resourceful and resilient, every single day. It's a system for capturing and using stories from your life to guide you in making the wise decisions that are right for you.

Dr Taryn Marie, an expert in resilience, reminds us about the value of our personal, lived experiences.

> 'Every experience that we have in our lives fundamentally and forever changes us in small, and large, ways. Therefore, once we've had an experience we don't go back to the way that we were before that experience. Resilience is about understanding, making meaning out of what is happening, what has happened, and allowing ourselves to be, again, fundamentally and forever changed in ways that allow us to be both more compassionate and empathetic, and to have more wisdom.'

You can tap into the wisdom of your past and present in times of change, to create the future you want to see. Not so you can tie the daily challenges that make up a life with a neat happily ever after bow, but so you can remind yourself that you have the answers you need to navigate the life you have and create the life you want to live.

*Our stories help us
to navigate change.*

Where do you turn when you don't know what to do?

GOOGLE
Gives you facts and information.

BOOKS
Give you information and knowledge.

EXPERTS
Give you knowledge, insights and opinions.

FRIENDS
Give you opinions based on their experiences.

YOUR HEART
Grants you intuition and insights based
on *your* experiences.

What if you could capture your wisest, strongest self to store away for a time when you need it the most?

Our decision-making processes are complex. We can't capture every factor that contributes to a decision in a single snapshot. We've developed mental shortcuts to make decisions in situations where we have complete information. It's not difficult to choose between tea or coffee, vanilla or chocolate. In many cases, though, there is no one right answer. It's a lot harder to make decisions you're happy with when you have incomplete information, when the emotional stakes are high, and time or resources are limited.

The ability to move forward with missing or limited information is a critical life skill.

Our memories and biases also come into play. From a young age, we understand that each decision has benefits and costs and that making decisions means living with the consequences of our choices. If a child spends all her pocket money on LEGO today, she knows she can't return to the store and buy books or art materials tomorrow.

We make decisions based on information and intuition using objective facts and unconscious emotional data. There is more to making good choices that align with our values than knowing the facts. For example, an investor, who also has strong feelings about protecting the environment, might ignore the hot tip on a mining stock because her values overrule her desire to grow her wealth.

The past is our patient teacher.

Our opinions, choices and actions are influenced by reason and emotion. It's easy to unearth facts. But there is valuable information to be gained from our lived experiences. They can help guide the decisions we make from the heart. Just because something isn't an objective fact doesn't mean it isn't valuable data. We sometimes overlook or ignore data from our past experiences because it's harder to find and recall.

We agonise about making the right decision. But maybe, the more important consideration is learning to trust yourself to make the decision that's *right for you?*

The experiences we live through teach us something about what we should do the next time we're faced with a challenge. Our stories help us to navigate change. We learn to love by having our hearts broken. We become better leaders by failing to lead. We are more resourceful when we discover our flaws. We develop resilience, not by staying upright, but by falling.

Our stories shape our beliefs about what's possible and remind us what we are capable of.

CREATING A
REFLECTION RITUAL

We don't get fit by reading about how to get fit. In the same way, what we write has a bigger impact on us than what we read. So where should we begin? Even if you already have a reflection ritual, you will benefit from using a system to get the most from the process. And if you don't, now is the best time to start. In this journal, I'll be sharing The Story Compass. This framework for reflecting helps you to choose an event or a small moment from your day, to record and learn from. In this way, your stories will become your guide. Think of it as a way to view your life using story as the lens.

Our reflection process will enable you to **recall, record, reframe** and **reset** your experiences. You will take snapshots of your life by looking for an out of the ordinary event or small moment in the day. Something that broke a pattern or made you stop and think. Recording these moments in story form will develop your insights and intuition, and reveal your capacity to be resourceful and resilient. As well as help you find moments of creativity, joy and gratitude and the foresight to make good decisions. The most exciting thing is that you will be the author of it all.

THE STORY COMPASS

When I teach people how to tell their personal or business stories, we use a framework to guide us.

For the purpose of reflection, I created a new simplified structure, The Story Compass. I've found it useful for remembering and reflecting on personal stories and events as a writer, coach, wife, mother, daughter and friend. You can use The Story Compass framework to help you to record and contextualise your stories, describing facts, thoughts, emotions and responses. You'll be breaking your stories into the following three stages:

CIRCUMSTANCES

Who. Where. When. What.

Your Reactions.

CHOICES

Your Alternatives.

CHANGE

Your Insights, Awareness and Responses.

"

At the center of your being you have the answer, you know who you are and you know what you want.

— LAO TZU

"

USING THE JOURNAL

This journal is perfect for evening reflection. You'll be using The Story Compass framework for recording your stories in a few short lines. The stories you choose to record don't need to be about a significant challenge in your life. You might also record small moments from your day or an unexpected happening that opened your eyes. These are your stories. Choose the one that stands out to you. There is no right or wrong answer. The goal is to get into the habit of recording your stories. So, with that in mind, I've given you limited space to outline your story. Of course, if you journal regularly, you might want to revisit a story and write more, but I've designed this journal to enable you to establish a habit, so that each entry can be completed in a few minutes.

On the following pages you'll see some examples of stories completed by people who have used the *A Compass for the Heart* journal.

DAY & DATE _____ 24th March 2019

CIRCUMSTANCES

Who/Where/When: It's my birthday and I'm at work. I haven't been part of this team for long and I don't mention that it's my birthday.

What happened? The team surprised me with a birthday cake that we shared for morning tea.

MY REACTIONS

What I felt: Surprised and happy. Closer to my colleagues.

What I thought: I wasn't expecting this. How did they know it was my birthday?

What I did: Thanked everyone and enjoyed the moment.

CHOICES

My alternatives: I could have dismissed this kind gesture and moved on with my day. But I chose to interpret the gesture as a sign that I was welcomed and valued by my new colleagues.

CHANGE

My insight, awareness and responses: I recognised that even though I have only been in this role for a short time that I am already a valued member of this team. That surprised me because I don't acknowledge my contribution as much as I should.

NOTE TO SELF

You are making a contribution and you are worthy of kindness. You belong.

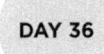

DAY & DATE _____ 15th May 2019

CIRCUMSTANCES

Who/Where/When: __A customer sent me an angry email today during__

the lockdown.

What happened? __He made a mistake and wanted me to bail him out.__

MY REACTIONS

What I felt: __Irritated, taken advantage of and put out. I was mad.__

What I thought: __Why should I help this guy? There is not much we can do__

with only half our company working right now.

What I did: __I decided to give him a call and tell him that we couldn't do__

what he wanted.

CHOICES

My alternatives: If this was a coaching client, how would I show up? I would get curious about what is going on in his world. Be interested in him. I would help him sort through his problem, without making it my problem. I would be an objective sounding board, not put out and irritated. I would help him uncover the real problem.

CHANGE

My insight, awareness and responses: On the call I discovered his world has turned upside down. His boss is breathing down his neck. I found a way to help him. Our company may be the only one in the country that can solve his problem. I shared the conversation with my team and we're excited to work on the problem.

NOTE TO SELF

The changes to my role have been disorienting. I haven't been enjoying my work. I can use my strengths to find meaning in this season and be a curious coach.

DAY & DATE _____ 12th June 2019

CIRCUMSTANCES

Who/Where/When: Sally suggested we take a hike with our daughters and the dogs today.

What happened? The loop we walk is about two miles. There are squirrel trails everywhere that Jenny wanted to go off and explore. I was up for it, but her older sister Rachel was annoyed. When we got lost Rachel started panicking, yelling and blaming at me.

MY REACTIONS

What I felt: I felt concerned and falsely accused and disrespected.

What I thought: We are a mile from our house. What's the big deal?

What I did: I got back to the main trail. Rachel stormed off alone.

CHOICES

My alternatives: Tell Rachel that she is being ridiculous and to get control of herself. Instead, I asked her why this bothered her so much. She said she felt unsafe on a trail she didn't know. Then the hardest one-that our family ignores her and her opinions don't matter.

CHANGE

My insight, awareness and responses: I told her I knew that feeling all too well, acknowledged that it's a horrible feeling and I don't want her to feel like that but sometimes it happens. Later, she apologised. She asked me to tell her about a time in my childhood when this happened. I shared my memories of being excited for my birthday as a kid and waking up to no presents, no cake and no nothing. At first, Rachel didn't believe me. Your parents are so rich. I acknowledged that they could have bought me anything. At that moment we connected and the little boy who wanted a new skateboard for his birthday felt that he was going to be okay.

NOTE TO SELF

I thought processing this stuff would get more comfortable by my 40's, but it is still hard sometimes. It has to be even harder for her at 18. I'm ready to step into it with her.

DAY & DATE _____ 16th August 2019

CIRCUMSTANCES

Who/Where/When: It's the first thing on Monday morning. I got a text from my friend Jo asking if I have time to call her. She needs help with a personal problem she's working through.

What happened? I looked in my diary and saw that the only time slot I could offer her was the hour I'd set aside to work on my podcast.

MY REACTIONS

What I felt: Conflicted I was torn between helping a friend and doing work that's important to me.

What I thought: I have a packed day. I don't want to do this.

What I did: I reminded myself about the times that Jo has been there for me. I rearranged my day and postponed a non-urgent meeting. Jo and I met for coffee.

CHOICES

My alternatives: I could have told Jo that I was too busy to see her today as I might have done that in the past. But today I intentionally chose to do the thing that is sometimes hard for me. I put a person I care about before a project I care about.

CHANGE

My insight, awareness and responses: Sometimes I make excuses to put projects before people because getting stuff done feels good. I don't get the satisfaction of ticking things off my to-do list when I have coffee with a friend because that doesn't belong on the to-do list. Maybe it should, because human connection makes me a better person.

NOTE TO SELF

I often measure success in terms of outcomes and achievements. There is more to a meaningful life than just getting things done.

*We think we tell
stories, but stories
often tell us.*

— REBECCA SOLNIT

OVER TO YOU

What will you learn from each story? The answer is, it depends. It depends on the telling, how deeply you want to reflect, and the lessons the story reveals to you over time. Perhaps you'll gain awareness of a story you're telling yourself—a narrative that is or isn't serving you. Maybe you'll get an insight into something that changes your thinking or behaviour. The goal is to allow the story to speak to you. Take what you need from it.

In the following pages, you'll find 90 blank Story Compass templates for you to date and record a story moment from your day and a *Reflection Ritual* checkbox for every 30 days where you can record each day you've completed a journal entry.

*The greatest
thing in the world is
to know how to
be yourself.*

— MICHEL DE MONTAIGNE

KEEPING TRACK

days 1 to 10

After you complete the journal entry for each of the days 1 to 10, come back here to note your progress by marking the circle for that day.

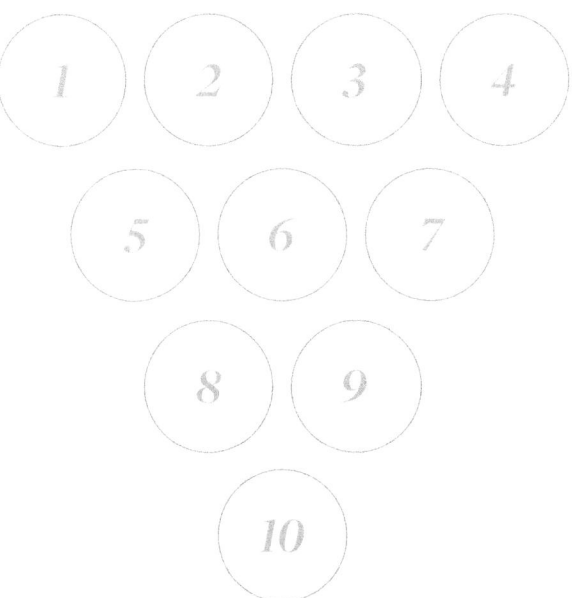

DAY 1   DAY & DATE _____

CIRCUMSTANCES

Who/Where/When: _____

_____

_____

_____

What happened? _____

_____

_____

_____

MY REACTIONS

What I felt: _____

_____

_____

What I thought: _____

_____

_____

What I did: _____

_____

_____

CHOICES

My alternatives:

_____

_____

_____

_____

_____

CHANGE

My insight, awareness and responses:

_____

_____

_____

_____

_____

_____

_____

_____

NOTE TO SELF

DAY 2   DAY & DATE _____

CIRCUMSTANCES

Who/Where/When: _____

_____

_____

_____

What happened? _____

_____

_____

_____

MY REACTIONS

What I felt: _____

_____

_____

What I thought: _____

_____

_____

What I did: _____

_____

_____

CHOICES

My alternatives:

_____

_____

_____

_____

_____

CHANGE

My insight, awareness and responses:

_____

_____

_____

_____

_____

_____

_____

_____

NOTE TO SELF

DAY & DATE _____

CIRCUMSTANCES

Who/Where/When: _____

_____

_____

_____

What happened? _____

_____

_____

_____

MY REACTIONS

What I felt: _____

_____

_____

What I thought: _____

_____

_____

What I did: _____

_____

_____

CHOICES

My alternatives:

_____

_____

_____

_____

_____

CHANGE

My insight, awareness and responses:

_____

_____

_____

_____

_____

_____

_____

_____

NOTE TO SELF

DAY 4   DAY & DATE _____

CIRCUMSTANCES

Who/Where/When: _____

_____

_____

_____

What happened? _____

_____

_____

_____

MY REACTIONS

What I felt: _____

_____

_____

What I thought: _____

_____

_____

What I did: _____

_____

_____

CHOICES

My alternatives:

_____

_____

_____

_____

_____

CHANGE

My insight, awareness and responses:

_____

_____

_____

_____

_____

_____

_____

_____

NOTE TO SELF

DAY 5 DAY & DATE _____

CIRCUMSTANCES

Who/Where/When: _____

_____

_____

_____

What happened? _____

_____

_____

_____

MY REACTIONS

What I felt: _____

_____

_____

What I thought: _____

_____

_____

What I did: _____

_____

_____

CHOICES

My alternatives: _____

_____

_____

_____

_____

CHANGE

My insight, awareness and responses: _____

_____

_____

_____

_____

_____

_____

_____

_____

_____

NOTE TO SELF

CIRCUMSTANCES

Who/Where/When: _____

_____

_____

_____

What happened? _____

_____

_____

_____

MY REACTIONS

What I felt: _____

_____

_____

What I thought: _____

_____

_____

What I did: _____

_____

_____

CHOICES

My alternatives:

_____

_____

_____

_____

_____

CHANGE

My insight, awareness and responses:

_____

_____

_____

_____

_____

_____

_____

_____

NOTE TO SELF

DAY 7 DAY & DATE _____

CIRCUMSTANCES

Who/Where/When: _____

_____

_____

_____

What happened? _____

_____

_____

_____

MY REACTIONS

What I felt: _____

_____

_____

What I thought: _____

_____

_____

What I did: _____

_____

_____

CHOICES

My alternatives:

_____

_____

_____

_____

_____

CHANGE

My insight, awareness and responses:

_____

_____

_____

_____

_____

_____

_____

_____

_____

NOTE TO SELF

DAY 8   DAY & DATE _____

CIRCUMSTANCES

Who/Where/When: _____

_____

_____

_____

What happened? _____

_____

_____

_____

MY REACTIONS

What I felt: _____

_____

_____

What I thought: _____

_____

_____

What I did: _____

_____

_____

CHOICES

My alternatives: _____

_____

_____

_____

_____

CHANGE

My insight, awareness and responses: _____

_____

_____

_____

_____

_____

_____

_____

NOTE TO SELF

DAY 9 DAY & DATE _____

CIRCUMSTANCES

Who/Where/When: _____

_____

_____

_____

What happened? _____

_____

_____

_____

MY REACTIONS

What I felt: _____

_____

_____

What I thought: _____

_____

_____

What I did: _____

_____

_____

CHOICES

My alternatives:

_____

_____

_____

_____

_____

CHANGE

My insight, awareness and responses:

_____

_____

_____

_____

_____

_____

_____

_____

_____

NOTE TO SELF

DAY 10   DAY & DATE _____

CIRCUMSTANCES

Who/Where/When: _____

_____

_____

_____

What happened? _____

_____

_____

_____

MY REACTIONS

What I felt: _____

_____

_____

What I thought: _____

_____

_____

What I did: _____

_____

_____

CHOICES

My alternatives:

_____

_____

_____

_____

_____

CHANGE

My insight, awareness and responses:

_____

_____

_____

_____

_____

_____

_____

_____

NOTE TO SELF

You get your intuition back when you make space for it.

— ANNE LAMOTT

KEEPING TRACK

days 11 to 20

After you complete the journal entry for each of the days 11 to 20, come back here to note your progress by marking the circle for that day.

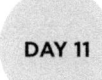

DAY 11   DAY & DATE _____

CIRCUMSTANCES

Who/Where/When: _____

_____

_____

_____

What happened? _____

_____

_____

_____

MY REACTIONS

What I felt: _____

_____

_____

What I thought: _____

_____

_____

What I did: _____

_____

_____

CHOICES

My alternatives:

_____

_____

_____

_____

_____

CHANGE

My insight, awareness and responses:

_____

_____

_____

_____

_____

_____

_____

_____

NOTE TO SELF

DAY 12   DAY & DATE _____

CIRCUMSTANCES

Who/Where/When: _____

_____

_____

_____

What happened? _____

_____

_____

_____

MY REACTIONS

What I felt: _____

_____

_____

What I thought: _____

_____

_____

What I did: _____

_____

_____

CHOICES

My alternatives:

_____

_____

_____

_____

_____

CHANGE

My insight, awareness and responses:

_____

_____

_____

_____

_____

_____

_____

NOTE TO SELF

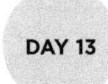

DAY & DATE _____

CIRCUMSTANCES

Who/Where/When: _____

_____

_____

_____

What happened? _____

_____

_____

_____

MY REACTIONS

What I felt: _____

_____

_____

What I thought: _____

_____

_____

What I did: _____

_____

_____

CHOICES

My alternatives: _____

_____

_____

_____

_____

CHANGE

My insight, awareness and responses: _____

_____

_____

_____

_____

_____

_____

_____

_____

_____

NOTE TO SELF

DAY 14 DAY & DATE _____

CIRCUMSTANCES

Who/Where/When: _____

_____

_____

_____

What happened? _____

_____

_____

_____

MY REACTIONS

What I felt: _____

_____

_____

What I thought: _____

_____

_____

What I did: _____

_____

_____

CHOICES

My alternatives:

_____

_____

_____

_____

_____

CHANGE

My insight, awareness and responses:

_____

_____

_____

_____

_____

_____

_____

_____

_____

NOTE TO SELF

DAY 15 DAY & DATE _____

CIRCUMSTANCES

Who/Where/When: _____

_____

_____

_____

What happened? _____

_____

_____

_____

MY REACTIONS

What I felt: _____

_____

_____

What I thought: _____

_____

_____

What I did: _____

_____

_____

CHOICES

My alternatives:

_____

_____

_____

_____

_____

CHANGE

My insight, awareness and responses:

_____

_____

_____

_____

_____

_____

_____

_____

NOTE TO SELF

DAY 16 DAY & DATE _____

CIRCUMSTANCES

Who/Where/When: _____

_____

_____

_____

What happened? _____

_____

_____

_____

MY REACTIONS

What I felt: _____

_____

_____

What I thought: _____

_____

_____

What I did: _____

_____

_____

CHOICES

My alternatives:

_____

_____

_____

_____

_____

CHANGE

My insight, awareness and responses:

_____

_____

_____

_____

_____

_____

_____

_____

NOTE TO SELF

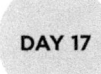

DAY 17   DAY & DATE _____

CIRCUMSTANCES

Who/Where/When: _____

_____

_____

_____

What happened? _____

_____

_____

_____

MY REACTIONS

What I felt: _____

_____

_____

What I thought: _____

_____

_____

What I did: _____

_____

_____

CHOICES

My alternatives:

_____

_____

_____

_____

CHANGE

My insight, awareness and responses:

_____

_____

_____

_____

_____

_____

_____

NOTE TO SELF

DAY 18 DAY & DATE _____

CIRCUMSTANCES

Who/Where/When: _____

_____

_____

_____

What happened? _____

_____

_____

_____

MY REACTIONS

What I felt: _____

_____

_____

What I thought: _____

_____

_____

What I did: _____

_____

_____

CHOICES

My alternatives:

_____

_____

_____

_____

_____

CHANGE

My insight, awareness and responses:

_____

_____

_____

_____

_____

_____

_____

_____

NOTE TO SELF

CIRCUMSTANCES

Who/Where/When: _____

_____

_____

_____

What happened? _____

_____

_____

_____

MY REACTIONS

What I felt: _____

_____

_____

What I thought: _____

_____

_____

What I did: _____

_____

_____

CHOICES

My alternatives: _____

_____

_____

_____

_____

_____

CHANGE

My insight, awareness and responses: _____

_____

_____

_____

_____

_____

_____

_____

_____

NOTE TO SELF

DAY & DATE _____

CIRCUMSTANCES

Who/Where/When: _____

_____

_____

_____

What happened? _____

_____

_____

_____

MY REACTIONS

What I felt: _____

_____

_____

What I thought: _____

_____

_____

What I did: _____

_____

_____

CHOICES

My alternatives: _____

_____

_____

_____

_____

CHANGE

My insight, awareness and responses: _____

_____

_____

_____

_____

_____

_____

_____

_____

NOTE TO SELF

The longest journey you will ever take is the 18 inches from your head to your heart.

— ANDREW BENNETT

KEEPING TRACK

days 21 to 30

After you complete the journal entry for each of the days 21 to 30, come back here to note your progress by marking the circle for that day.

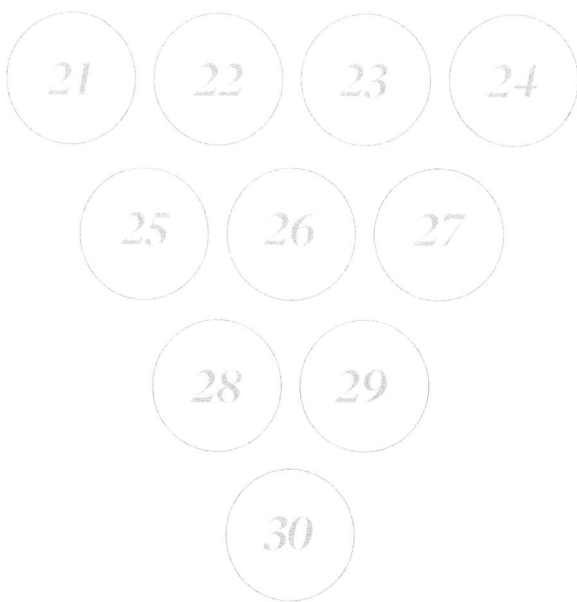

DAY 21　DAY & DATE _____

CIRCUMSTANCES

Who/Where/When: _____

_____

_____

_____

What happened? _____

_____

_____

_____

MY REACTIONS

What I felt: _____

_____

_____

What I thought: _____

_____

_____

What I did: _____

_____

_____

CHOICES

My alternatives:

_____

_____

_____

_____

_____

CHANGE

My insight, awareness and responses:

_____

_____

_____

_____

_____

_____

_____

_____

_____

NOTE TO SELF

DAY 22　　DAY & DATE _____

CIRCUMSTANCES

Who/Where/When: _____

_____

_____

_____

What happened? _____

_____

_____

_____

MY REACTIONS

What I felt: _____

_____

_____

What I thought: _____

_____

_____

What I did: _____

_____

_____

CHOICES

My alternatives:

_____

_____

_____

_____

_____

CHANGE

My insight, awareness and responses:

_____

_____

_____

_____

_____

_____

_____

_____

NOTE TO SELF

DAY 23   DAY & DATE _____

CIRCUMSTANCES

Who/Where/When: _____

_____

_____

_____

What happened? _____

_____

_____

_____

MY REACTIONS

What I felt: _____

_____

_____

What I thought: _____

_____

_____

What I did: _____

_____

_____

CHOICES

My alternatives:

_____

_____

_____

_____

_____

CHANGE

My insight, awareness and responses:

_____

_____

_____

_____

_____

_____

_____

_____

NOTE TO SELF

DAY & DATE _____

CIRCUMSTANCES

Who/Where/When: _____

_____

_____

_____

What happened? _____

_____

_____

_____

MY REACTIONS

What I felt: _____

_____

_____

What I thought: _____

_____

_____

What I did: _____

_____

_____

CHOICES

My alternatives: _____

_____

_____

_____

_____

CHANGE

My insight, awareness and responses: _____

_____

_____

_____

_____

_____

_____

_____

_____

NOTE TO SELF

DAY 25 DAY & DATE _____

CIRCUMSTANCES

Who/Where/When: _____

_____

_____

_____

What happened? _____

_____

_____

_____

MY REACTIONS

What I felt: _____

_____

_____

What I thought: _____

_____

_____

What I did: _____

_____

_____

CHOICES

My alternatives: _____

_____

_____

_____

_____

CHANGE

My insight, awareness and responses: _____

_____

_____

_____

_____

_____

_____

_____

_____

NOTE TO SELF

DAY & DATE _____

CIRCUMSTANCES

Who/Where/When: _____

_____

_____

_____

What happened? _____

_____

_____

_____

MY REACTIONS

What I felt: _____

_____

_____

What I thought: _____

_____

_____

What I did: _____

_____

_____

CHOICES

My alternatives:

_____

_____

_____

_____

_____

CHANGE

My insight, awareness and responses:

_____

_____

_____

_____

_____

_____

_____

_____

_____

_____

_____

NOTE TO SELF

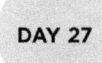

DAY 27 DAY & DATE _____

CIRCUMSTANCES

Who/Where/When: _____

_____

_____

_____

What happened? _____

_____

_____

_____

MY REACTIONS

What I felt: _____

_____

_____

What I thought: _____

_____

_____

What I did: _____

_____

_____

CHOICES

My alternatives: _____

_____

_____

_____

_____

CHANGE

My insight, awareness and responses: _____

_____

_____

_____

_____

_____

_____

_____

NOTE TO SELF

DAY 28 DAY & DATE _____

CIRCUMSTANCES

Who/Where/When: _____

_____

_____

_____

What happened? _____

_____

_____

_____

MY REACTIONS

What I felt: _____

_____

_____

What I thought: _____

_____

_____

What I did: _____

_____

_____

CHOICES

My alternatives:

_____

_____

_____

_____

_____

CHANGE

My insight, awareness and responses:

_____

_____

_____

_____

_____

_____

_____

_____

NOTE TO SELF

DAY 29

DAY & DATE _____

CIRCUMSTANCES

Who/Where/When: _____

_____

_____

_____

What happened? _____

_____

_____

_____

MY REACTIONS

What I felt: _____

_____

_____

What I thought: _____

_____

_____

What I did: _____

_____

_____

CHOICES

My alternatives:

_____

_____

_____

_____

_____

CHANGE

My insight, awareness and responses:

_____

_____

_____

_____

_____

_____

_____

_____

NOTE TO SELF

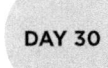

DAY 30   DAY & DATE _____

CIRCUMSTANCES

Who/Where/When: _____

_____

_____

_____

What happened? _____

_____

_____

_____

MY REACTIONS

What I felt: _____

_____

_____

What I thought: _____

_____

_____

What I did: _____

_____

_____

CHOICES

My alternatives: _____

_____

_____

_____

_____

CHANGE

My insight, awareness and responses: _____

_____

_____

_____

_____

_____

_____

_____

NOTE TO SELF

*Whatever happens
to you belongs to you.
Make it yours.
Feed it to yourself
even if it feels
impossible to swallow.
Let it nurture you,
because it will.*

— CHERYL STRAYED

KEEPING TRACK
days 31 to 40

After you complete the journal entry for each of the days 31 to 40, come back here to note your progress by marking the circle for that day.

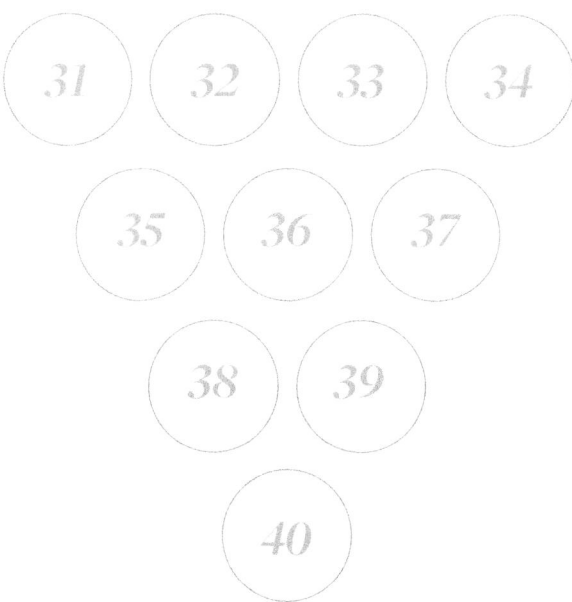

DAY 31 DAY & DATE _____

CIRCUMSTANCES

Who/Where/When: _____

_____

_____

_____

What happened? _____

_____

_____

_____

MY REACTIONS

What I felt: _____

_____

_____

What I thought: _____

_____

_____

What I did: _____

_____

_____

CHOICES

My alternatives:

CHANGE

My insight, awareness and responses:

DAY & DATE _____

CIRCUMSTANCES

Who/Where/When: _____

_____

_____

_____

What happened? _____

_____

_____

_____

MY REACTIONS

What I felt: _____

_____

_____

What I thought: _____

_____

_____

What I did: _____

_____

_____

CHOICES

My alternatives: _____

_____

_____

_____

_____

CHANGE

My insight, awareness and responses: _____

_____

_____

_____

_____

_____

_____

_____

_____

NOTE TO SELF

DAY 33   DAY & DATE _____

CIRCUMSTANCES

Who/Where/When: _____

_____

_____

_____

What happened? _____

_____

_____

_____

MY REACTIONS

What I felt: _____

_____

_____

What I thought: _____

_____

_____

What I did: _____

_____

_____

CHOICES

My alternatives:

_____

_____

_____

_____

_____

CHANGE

My insight, awareness and responses:

_____

_____

_____

_____

_____

_____

_____

_____

_____

_____

NOTE TO SELF

DAY 34   DAY & DATE _____

CIRCUMSTANCES

Who/Where/When: _____

_____

_____

_____

What happened? _____

_____

_____

_____

MY REACTIONS

What I felt: _____

_____

_____

What I thought: _____

_____

_____

What I did: _____

_____

_____

CHOICES

My alternatives: _____

_____

_____

_____

_____

CHANGE

My insight, awareness and responses: _____

_____

_____

_____

_____

_____

_____

_____

_____

DAY & DATE _____

CIRCUMSTANCES

Who/Where/When: _____

_____

_____

_____

What happened? _____

_____

_____

_____

MY REACTIONS

What I felt: _____

_____

_____

What I thought: _____

_____

_____

What I did: _____

_____

_____

CHOICES

My alternatives: _____

_____

_____

_____

_____

CHANGE

My insight, awareness and responses: _____

_____

_____

_____

_____

_____

_____

_____

_____

—————————————— NOTE TO SELF ——————————————

DAY & DATE _____

CIRCUMSTANCES

Who/Where/When: _____

_____

_____

_____

What happened? _____

_____

_____

_____

MY REACTIONS

What I felt: _____

_____

_____

What I thought: _____

_____

_____

What I did: _____

_____

_____

CHOICES

My alternatives:

_____

_____

_____

_____

_____

CHANGE

My insight, awareness and responses:

_____

_____

_____

_____

_____

_____

_____

_____

NOTE TO SELF

DAY & DATE _____

CIRCUMSTANCES

Who/Where/When: _____

_____

_____

_____

What happened? _____

_____

_____

_____

MY REACTIONS

What I felt: _____

_____

_____

What I thought: _____

_____

_____

What I did: _____

_____

_____

CHOICES

My alternatives:

_____

_____

_____

_____

_____

CHANGE

My insight, awareness and responses:

_____

_____

_____

_____

_____

_____

_____

_____

NOTE TO SELF

DAY & DATE _____

CIRCUMSTANCES

Who/Where/When: _____

_____

_____

_____

What happened? _____

_____

_____

_____

MY REACTIONS

What I felt: _____

_____

_____

What I thought: _____

_____

_____

What I did: _____

_____

_____

CHOICES

My alternatives:

_____

_____

_____

_____

_____

CHANGE

My insight, awareness and responses:

_____

_____

_____

_____

_____

_____

_____

_____

NOTE TO SELF

DAY & DATE _____

CIRCUMSTANCES

Who/Where/When: _____

_____

_____

_____

What happened? _____

_____

_____

_____

MY REACTIONS

What I felt: _____

_____

_____

What I thought: _____

_____

_____

What I did: _____

_____

_____

CHOICES

My alternatives:

_____

_____

_____

_____

_____

CHANGE

My insight, awareness and responses:

_____

_____

_____

_____

_____

_____

_____

_____

_____

NOTE TO SELF

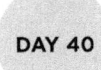

DAY 40   DAY & DATE _____

CIRCUMSTANCES

Who/Where/When: _____

_____

_____

_____

What happened? _____

_____

_____

_____

MY REACTIONS

What I felt: _____

_____

_____

What I thought: _____

_____

_____

What I did: _____

_____

_____

CHOICES

My alternatives: _____

_____

_____

_____

_____

CHANGE

My insight, awareness and responses: _____

_____

_____

_____

_____

_____

_____

_____

_____

_____

NOTE TO SELF

The world spins.
We stumble on.
It is enough.

— COLUM MCCANN

KEEPING TRACK

days 41 to 50

After you complete the journal entry for each of the days 41 to 50, come back here to note your progress by marking the circle for that day.

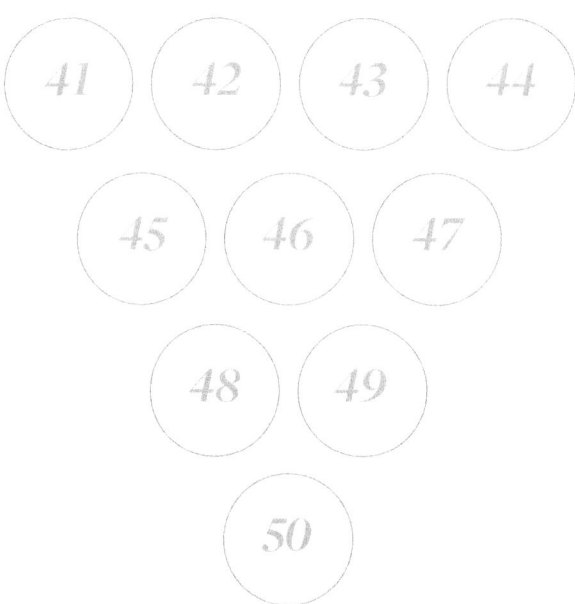

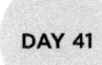

DAY 41 DAY & DATE _____

CIRCUMSTANCES

Who/Where/When: _____

_____

_____

_____

What happened? _____

_____

_____

_____

MY REACTIONS

What I felt: _____

_____

_____

What I thought: _____

_____

_____

What I did: _____

_____

_____

CHOICES

My alternatives: _____

_____

_____

_____

_____

CHANGE

My insight, awareness and responses: _____

_____

_____

_____

_____

_____

_____

_____

_____

NOTE TO SELF

DAY & DATE _____

CIRCUMSTANCES

Who/Where/When: _____

_____

_____

_____

What happened? _____

_____

_____

_____

MY REACTIONS

What I felt: _____

_____

_____

What I thought: _____

_____

_____

What I did: _____

_____

_____

CHOICES

My alternatives:

_____

_____

_____

_____

_____

CHANGE

My insight, awareness and responses:

_____

_____

_____

_____

_____

_____

_____

_____

NOTE TO SELF

DAY & DATE _____

CIRCUMSTANCES

Who/Where/When: _____

_____

_____

_____

What happened? _____

_____

_____

_____

MY REACTIONS

What I felt: _____

_____

_____

What I thought: _____

_____

_____

What I did: _____

_____

_____

CHOICES

My alternatives:

_____

_____

_____

_____

_____

CHANGE

My insight, awareness and responses:

_____

_____

_____

_____

_____

_____

_____

_____

NOTE TO SELF

DAY 44 DAY & DATE _____

CIRCUMSTANCES

Who/Where/When: _____

_____

_____

_____

What happened? _____

_____

_____

_____

MY REACTIONS

What I felt: _____

_____

_____

What I thought: _____

_____

_____

What I did: _____

_____

_____

CHOICES

My alternatives:

_____

_____

_____

_____

_____

CHANGE

My insight, awareness and responses:

_____

_____

_____

_____

_____

_____

_____

_____

_____

NOTE TO SELF

DAY 45 DAY & DATE _____

CIRCUMSTANCES

Who/Where/When: _____

_____

_____

_____

What happened? _____

_____

_____

_____

MY REACTIONS

What I felt: _____

_____

_____

What I thought: _____

_____

_____

What I did: _____

_____

_____

CHOICES

My alternatives:

_____

_____

_____

_____

_____

CHANGE

My insight, awareness and responses:

_____

_____

_____

_____

_____

_____

_____

_____

NOTE TO SELF

DAY & DATE _____

CIRCUMSTANCES

Who/Where/When: _____

_____

_____

_____

What happened? _____

_____

_____

_____

MY REACTIONS

What I felt: _____

_____

_____

What I thought: _____

_____

_____

What I did: _____

_____

_____

CHOICES

My alternatives:

_____

_____

_____

_____

CHANGE

My insight, awareness and responses:

_____

_____

_____

_____

_____

_____

_____

_____

NOTE TO SELF

DAY 47 DAY & DATE _____

CIRCUMSTANCES

Who/Where/When: _____

_____

_____

_____

What happened? _____

_____

_____

_____

MY REACTIONS

What I felt: _____

_____

_____

What I thought: _____

_____

_____

What I did: _____

_____

_____

CHOICES

My alternatives:

_____

_____

_____

_____

_____

CHANGE

My insight, awareness and responses:

_____

_____

_____

_____

_____

_____

_____

_____

_____

NOTE TO SELF

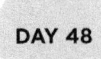

DAY 48 DAY & DATE _____

CIRCUMSTANCES

Who/Where/When: _____

_____

_____

_____

What happened? _____

_____

_____

_____

MY REACTIONS

What I felt: _____

_____

_____

What I thought: _____

_____

_____

What I did: _____

_____

_____

CHOICES

My alternatives: _____

_____

_____

_____

_____

CHANGE

My insight, awareness and responses: _____

_____

_____

_____

_____

_____

_____

_____

_____

-------------------- NOTE TO SELF --------------------

DAY & DATE _____

CIRCUMSTANCES

Who/Where/When: _____

_____

_____

_____

What happened? _____

_____

_____

_____

MY REACTIONS

What I felt: _____

_____

_____

What I thought: _____

_____

_____

What I did: _____

_____

_____

CHOICES

My alternatives:

_____

_____

_____

_____

CHANGE

My insight, awareness and responses:

_____

_____

_____

_____

_____

_____

_____

_____

NOTE TO SELF

DAY 50 DAY & DATE _____

CIRCUMSTANCES

Who/Where/When: _____

_____

_____

_____

What happened? _____

_____

_____

_____

MY REACTIONS

What I felt: _____

_____

_____

What I thought: _____

_____

_____

What I did: _____

_____

_____

CHOICES

My alternatives: _____

_____

_____

_____

_____

CHANGE

My insight, awareness and responses: _____

_____

_____

_____

_____

_____

_____

_____

_____

NOTE TO SELF

"

Not I, nor anyone else can travel that road for you. You must travel it by yourself. It is not far. It is within reach.

— WALT WHITMAN

"

KEEPING TRACK
days 51 to 60

After you complete the journal entry for each of the days 51 to 60, come back here to note your progress by marking the circle for that day.

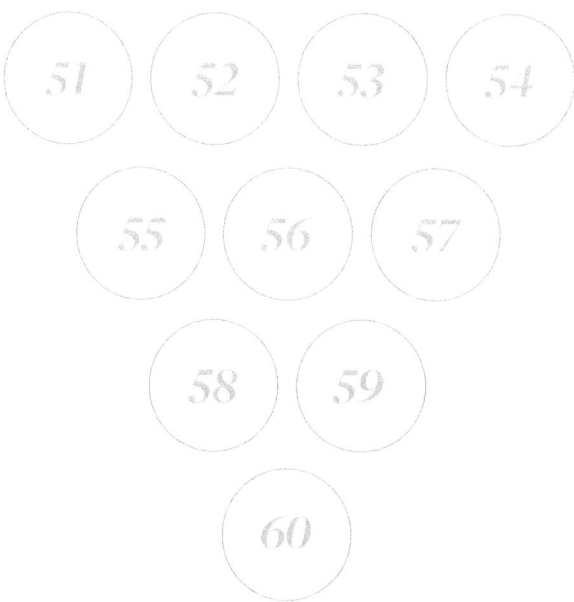

DAY 51 DAY & DATE _____

CIRCUMSTANCES

Who/Where/When: _____

_____

_____

_____

What happened? _____

_____

_____

_____

MY REACTIONS

What I felt: _____

_____

_____

What I thought: _____

_____

_____

What I did: _____

_____

_____

CHOICES

My alternatives: _____

_____

_____

_____

_____

CHANGE

My insight, awareness and responses: _____

_____

_____

_____

_____

_____

_____

_____

NOTE TO SELF

DAY 52 DAY & DATE _____

CIRCUMSTANCES

Who/Where/When: _____

_____

_____

_____

What happened? _____

_____

_____

_____

MY REACTIONS

What I felt: _____

_____

_____

What I thought: _____

_____

_____

What I did: _____

_____

_____

CHOICES

My alternatives:

_____

_____

_____

_____

_____

CHANGE

My insight, awareness and responses:

_____

_____

_____

_____

_____

_____

_____

_____

NOTE TO SELF

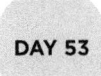 **DAY 53** DAY & DATE _____

CIRCUMSTANCES

Who/Where/When: _____

_____

_____

_____

What happened? _____

_____

_____

_____

MY REACTIONS

What I felt: _____

_____

_____

What I thought: _____

_____

_____

What I did: _____

_____

_____

CHOICES

My alternatives:

_____

_____

_____

_____

_____

CHANGE

My insight, awareness and responses:

_____

_____

_____

_____

_____

_____

_____

_____

_____

NOTE TO SELF

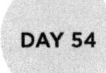

DAY 54   DAY & DATE _____

CIRCUMSTANCES

Who/Where/When: _____

_____

_____

_____

What happened? _____

_____

_____

_____

MY REACTIONS

What I felt: _____

_____

_____

What I thought: _____

_____

_____

What I did: _____

_____

_____

CHOICES

My alternatives:

_____

_____

_____

_____

_____

CHANGE

My insight, awareness and responses:

_____

_____

_____

_____

_____

_____

_____

_____

NOTE TO SELF

DAY & DATE _____

CIRCUMSTANCES

Who/Where/When: _____

_____

_____

_____

What happened? _____

_____

_____

_____

MY REACTIONS

What I felt: _____

_____

_____

What I thought: _____

_____

_____

What I did: _____

_____

_____

CHOICES

My alternatives:

_____

_____

_____

_____

_____

CHANGE

My insight, awareness and responses:

_____

_____

_____

_____

_____

_____

_____

_____

_____

NOTE TO SELF

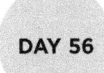

DAY 56　DAY & DATE _____

CIRCUMSTANCES

Who/Where/When: _____

_____

_____

_____

What happened? _____

_____

_____

_____

MY REACTIONS

What I felt: _____

_____

_____

What I thought: _____

_____

_____

What I did: _____

_____

_____

CHOICES

My alternatives:

CHANGE

My insight, awareness and responses:

NOTE TO SELF

DAY & DATE _____

CIRCUMSTANCES

Who/Where/When: _____

_____

_____

_____

What happened? _____

_____

_____

_____

MY REACTIONS

What I felt: _____

_____

_____

What I thought: _____

_____

_____

What I did: _____

_____

_____

CHOICES

My alternatives: _____

_____

_____

_____

_____

CHANGE

My insight, awareness and responses: _____

_____

_____

_____

_____

_____

_____

_____

NOTE TO SELF

DAY & DATE _____

CIRCUMSTANCES

Who/Where/When: _____

_____

_____

_____

What happened? _____

_____

_____

_____

MY REACTIONS

What I felt: _____

_____

_____

What I thought: _____

_____

_____

What I did: _____

_____

_____

CHOICES

My alternatives:

_____

_____

_____

_____

_____

CHANGE

My insight, awareness and responses:

_____

_____

_____

_____

_____

_____

_____

_____

NOTE TO SELF

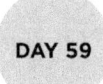

DAY 59 DAY & DATE _____

CIRCUMSTANCES

Who/Where/When: _____

_____

_____

_____

_____

What happened? _____

_____

_____

_____

MY REACTIONS

What I felt: _____

_____

_____

What I thought: _____

_____

_____

What I did: _____

_____

_____

CHOICES

My alternatives: _____

_____

_____

_____

_____

CHANGE

My insight, awareness and responses: _____

_____

_____

_____

_____

_____

_____

_____

_____

_____

NOTE TO SELF

DAY 60   DAY & DATE _____

CIRCUMSTANCES

Who/Where/When: _____

_____

_____

_____

What happened? _____

_____

_____

_____

MY REACTIONS

What I felt: _____

_____

_____

What I thought: _____

_____

_____

What I did: _____

_____

_____

CHOICES

My alternatives:

_____

_____

_____

_____

_____

CHANGE

My insight, awareness and responses:

_____

_____

_____

_____

_____

_____

_____

_____

_____

NOTE TO SELF

*Knowing yourself
is the beginning of
all wisdom.*

— ARISTOTLE

KEEPING TRACK

days 61 to 70

After you complete the journal entry for each of the days 61 to 70, come back here to note your progress by marking the circle for that day.

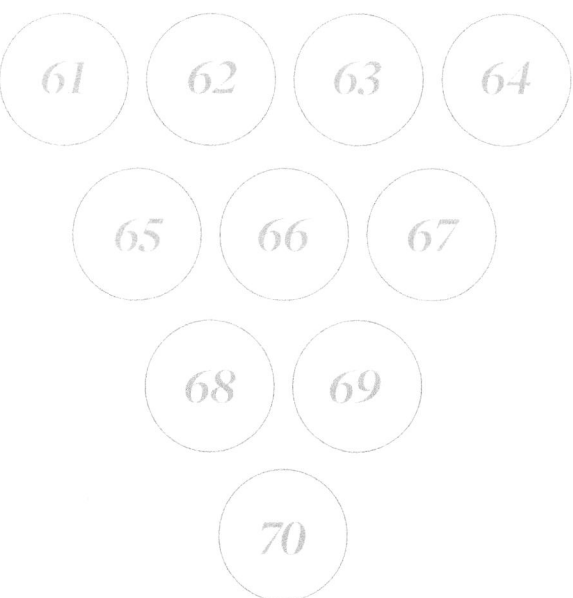

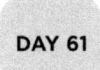

DAY 61

DAY & DATE _____

CIRCUMSTANCES

Who/Where/When: _____

_____

_____

_____

What happened? _____

_____

_____

_____

MY REACTIONS

What I felt: _____

_____

_____

What I thought: _____

_____

_____

What I did: _____

_____

_____

CHOICES

My alternatives:

_____

_____

_____

_____

_____

CHANGE

My insight, awareness and responses:

_____

_____

_____

_____

_____

_____

_____

_____

NOTE TO SELF

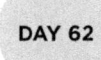

DAY 62 DAY & DATE _____

CIRCUMSTANCES

Who/Where/When: _____

_____

_____

_____

What happened? _____

_____

_____

_____

MY REACTIONS

What I felt: _____

_____

_____

What I thought: _____

_____

_____

What I did: _____

_____

_____

CHOICES

My alternatives: _____

_____

_____

_____

_____

CHANGE

My insight, awareness and responses: _____

_____

_____

_____

_____

_____

_____

_____

NOTE TO SELF

DAY & DATE _____

CIRCUMSTANCES

Who/Where/When: _____

_____

_____

_____

What happened? _____

_____

_____

_____

MY REACTIONS

What I felt: _____

_____

_____

_____

What I thought: _____

_____

_____

_____

What I did: _____

_____

_____

_____

CHOICES

My alternatives:

_____

_____

_____

_____

_____

CHANGE

My insight, awareness and responses:

_____

_____

_____

_____

_____

_____

_____

_____

_____

_____

NOTE TO SELF

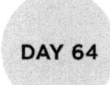

DAY 64

DAY & DATE _____

CIRCUMSTANCES

Who/Where/When: _____

_____

_____

_____

What happened? _____

_____

_____

_____

MY REACTIONS

What I felt: _____

_____

_____

What I thought: _____

_____

_____

What I did: _____

_____

_____

CHOICES

My alternatives:

_____

_____

_____

_____

CHANGE

My insight, awareness and responses:

_____

_____

_____

_____

_____

_____

_____

_____

NOTE TO SELF

DAY & DATE _____

CIRCUMSTANCES

Who/Where/When: _____

_____

_____

_____

What happened? _____

_____

_____

_____

MY REACTIONS

What I felt: _____

_____

_____

What I thought: _____

_____

_____

What I did: _____

_____

_____

CHOICES

My alternatives: _____

_____

_____

_____

_____

CHANGE

My insight, awareness and responses: _____

_____

_____

_____

_____

_____

_____

_____

NOTE TO SELF

DAY 66   DAY & DATE _____

CIRCUMSTANCES

Who/Where/When: _____

_____

_____

_____

What happened? _____

_____

_____

_____

MY REACTIONS

What I felt: _____

_____

_____

What I thought: _____

_____

_____

What I did: _____

_____

_____

CHOICES

My alternatives:

_____

_____

_____

_____

_____

CHANGE

My insight, awareness and responses:

_____

_____

_____

_____

_____

_____

_____

_____

NOTE TO SELF

DAY 67

DAY & DATE _____

CIRCUMSTANCES

Who/Where/When: _____

_____

_____

_____

What happened? _____

_____

_____

_____

MY REACTIONS

What I felt: _____

_____

_____

What I thought: _____

_____

_____

What I did: _____

_____

_____

CHOICES

My alternatives:

_____

_____

_____

_____

_____

CHANGE

My insight, awareness and responses:

_____

_____

_____

_____

_____

_____

_____

_____

NOTE TO SELF

DAY & DATE _____

CIRCUMSTANCES

Who/Where/When: _____

_____

_____

_____

What happened? _____

_____

_____

_____

MY REACTIONS

What I felt: _____

_____

_____

What I thought: _____

_____

_____

What I did: _____

_____

_____

CHOICES

My alternatives:

_____

_____

_____

_____

_____

CHANGE

My insight, awareness and responses:

_____

_____

_____

_____

_____

_____

_____

_____

NOTE TO SELF

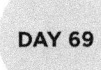

DAY 69 DAY & DATE _____

CIRCUMSTANCES

Who/Where/When: _____

_____

_____

_____

What happened? _____

_____

_____

_____

MY REACTIONS

What I felt: _____

_____

_____

What I thought: _____

_____

_____

What I did: _____

_____

_____

CHOICES

My alternatives:

_____

_____

_____

_____

_____

CHANGE

My insight, awareness and responses:

_____

_____

_____

_____

_____

_____

_____

_____

NOTE TO SELF

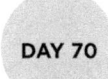

DAY 70   DAY & DATE _____

CIRCUMSTANCES

Who/Where/When: _____

_____

_____

_____

What happened? _____

_____

_____

_____

MY REACTIONS

What I felt: _____

_____

_____

What I thought: _____

_____

_____

What I did: _____

_____

_____

CHOICES

My alternatives:

_____

_____

_____

_____

_____

CHANGE

My insight, awareness and responses:

_____

_____

_____

_____

_____

_____

_____

_____

NOTE TO SELF

Have the courage to follow your heart and intuition. They somehow already know what you truly want to become.

— STEVE JOBS

KEEPING TRACK
days 71 to 80

After you complete the journal entry for each of the days 71 to 80, come back here to note your progress by marking the circle for that day.

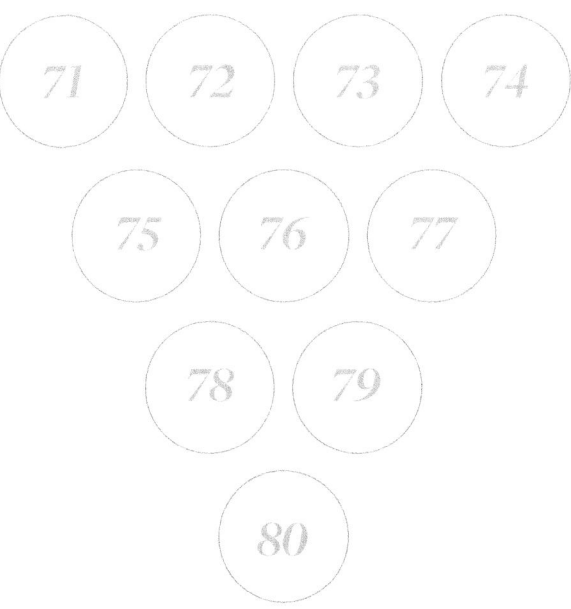

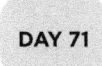

DAY 71   DAY & DATE _____

CIRCUMSTANCES

Who/Where/When: _____

_____

_____

_____

What happened? _____

_____

_____

_____

MY REACTIONS

What I felt: _____

_____

_____

What I thought: _____

_____

_____

What I did: _____

_____

_____

CHOICES

My alternatives: _____

_____

_____

_____

_____

CHANGE

My insight, awareness and responses: _____

_____

_____

_____

_____

_____

_____

_____

_____

NOTE TO SELF

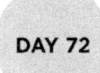

DAY 72   DAY & DATE _____

CIRCUMSTANCES

Who/Where/When: _____

_____

_____

_____

What happened? _____

_____

_____

_____

MY REACTIONS

What I felt: _____

_____

_____

What I thought: _____

_____

_____

What I did: _____

_____

_____

CHOICES

My alternatives:

_____

_____

_____

_____

_____

CHANGE

My insight, awareness and responses:

_____

_____

_____

_____

_____

_____

_____

_____

NOTE TO SELF

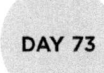

DAY 73   DAY & DATE _____

CIRCUMSTANCES

Who/Where/When: _____

_____

_____

_____

What happened? _____

_____

_____

_____

MY REACTIONS

What I felt: _____

_____

_____

What I thought: _____

_____

_____

What I did: _____

_____

_____

CHOICES

My alternatives: _____

_____

_____

_____

_____

CHANGE

My insight, awareness and responses: _____

_____

_____

_____

_____

_____

_____

_____

_____

--- NOTE TO SELF ---

DAY & DATE _____

CIRCUMSTANCES

Who/Where/When: _____

_____

_____

_____

What happened? _____

_____

_____

_____

MY REACTIONS

What I felt: _____

_____

_____

What I thought: _____

_____

_____

What I did: _____

_____

_____

CHOICES

My alternatives:

_____

_____

_____

_____

_____

CHANGE

My insight, awareness and responses:

_____

_____

_____

_____

_____

_____

_____

_____

_____

NOTE TO SELF

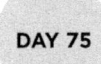 **DAY 75** DAY & DATE _____

CIRCUMSTANCES

Who/Where/When: _____

_____

_____

_____

What happened? _____

_____

_____

_____

MY REACTIONS

What I felt: _____

_____

_____

What I thought: _____

_____

_____

What I did: _____

_____

_____

CHOICES

My alternatives:

CHANGE

My insight, awareness and responses:

NOTE TO SELF

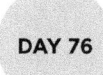

DAY & DATE _____

CIRCUMSTANCES

Who/Where/When: _____

_____

_____

_____

What happened? _____

_____

_____

_____

MY REACTIONS

What I felt: _____

_____

_____

What I thought: _____

_____

_____

What I did: _____

_____

_____

CHOICES

My alternatives:

_____

_____

_____

_____

_____

CHANGE

My insight, awareness and responses:

_____

_____

_____

_____

_____

_____

_____

_____

NOTE TO SELF

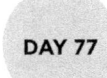

DAY 77 DAY & DATE _____

CIRCUMSTANCES

Who/Where/When: _____

_____

_____

_____

What happened? _____

_____

_____

_____

MY REACTIONS

What I felt: _____

_____

_____

What I thought: _____

_____

_____

What I did: _____

_____

_____

CHOICES

My alternatives:

_____

_____

_____

_____

_____

CHANGE

My insight, awareness and responses:

_____

_____

_____

_____

_____

_____

_____

_____

NOTE TO SELF

DAY 78   DAY & DATE _____

CIRCUMSTANCES

Who/Where/When: _____

_____

_____

_____

What happened? _____

_____

_____

_____

MY REACTIONS

What I felt: _____

_____

_____

What I thought: _____

_____

_____

What I did: _____

_____

_____

CHOICES

My alternatives:

_____

_____

_____

_____

_____

_____

CHANGE

My insight, awareness and responses:

_____

_____

_____

_____

_____

_____

_____

_____

_____

NOTE TO SELF

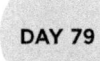

DAY 79 DAY & DATE _____

CIRCUMSTANCES

Who/Where/When: _____

_____

_____

_____

What happened? _____

_____

_____

_____

MY REACTIONS

What I felt: _____

_____

_____

What I thought: _____

_____

_____

What I did: _____

_____

_____

CHOICES

My alternatives: _____

_____

_____

_____

_____

CHANGE

My insight, awareness and responses: _____

_____

_____

_____

_____

_____

_____

_____

_____

DAY 80   DAY & DATE _____

CIRCUMSTANCES

Who/Where/When: _____

_____

_____

_____

What happened? _____

_____

_____

_____

MY REACTIONS

What I felt: _____

_____

_____

What I thought: _____

_____

_____

What I did: _____

_____

_____

CHOICES

My alternatives:

_____

_____

_____

_____

_____

CHANGE

My insight, awareness and responses:

_____

_____

_____

_____

_____

_____

_____

_____

_____

NOTE TO SELF

You will never follow your own inner voice until you clear up the doubts in your mind.

— ROY T. BENNETT

KEEPING TRACK

days 81 to 90

After you complete the journal entry for each of the days 81 to 90, come back here to note your progress by marking the circle for that day.

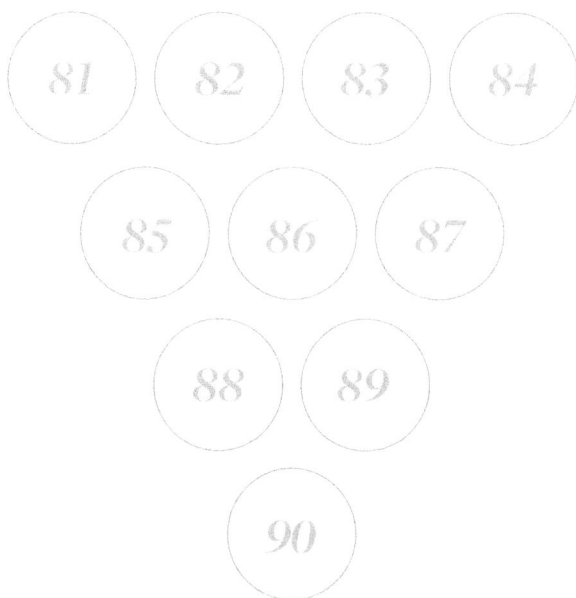

DAY & DATE _____

CIRCUMSTANCES

Who/Where/When: _____

_____

_____

_____

What happened? _____

_____

_____

_____

MY REACTIONS

What I felt: _____

_____

_____

What I thought: _____

_____

_____

What I did: _____

_____

_____

CHOICES

My alternatives: _____

_____

_____

_____

_____

CHANGE

My insight, awareness and responses: _____

_____

_____

_____

_____

_____

_____

_____

--- NOTE TO SELF ---

DAY 82   DAY & DATE _____

CIRCUMSTANCES

Who/Where/When: _____

_____

_____

_____

What happened? _____

_____

_____

_____

MY REACTIONS

What I felt: _____

_____

_____

What I thought: _____

_____

_____

What I did: _____

_____

_____

CHOICES

My alternatives:

_____

_____

_____

_____

_____

CHANGE

My insight, awareness and responses:

_____

_____

_____

_____

_____

_____

_____

_____

_____

NOTE TO SELF

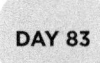

DAY 83   DAY & DATE _____

CIRCUMSTANCES

Who/Where/When: _____

_____

_____

_____

What happened? _____

_____

_____

_____

MY REACTIONS

What I felt: _____

_____

_____

What I thought: _____

_____

_____

What I did: _____

_____

_____

CHOICES

My alternatives:

_____

_____

_____

_____

CHANGE

My insight, awareness and responses:

_____

_____

_____

_____

_____

_____

_____

_____

NOTE TO SELF

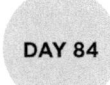

DAY 84 DAY & DATE _____

CIRCUMSTANCES

Who/Where/When: _____

_____

_____

_____

What happened? _____

_____

_____

_____

MY REACTIONS

What I felt: _____

_____

_____

What I thought: _____

_____

_____

What I did: _____

_____

_____

CHOICES

My alternatives: _____

_____

_____

_____

_____

CHANGE

My insight, awareness and responses: _____

_____

_____

_____

_____

_____

_____

_____

_____

NOTE TO SELF

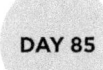

DAY 85   DAY & DATE _____

CIRCUMSTANCES

Who/Where/When: _____

_____

_____

_____

What happened? _____

_____

_____

_____

MY REACTIONS

What I felt: _____

_____

_____

What I thought: _____

_____

_____

What I did: _____

_____

_____

CHOICES

My alternatives: _____

_____

_____

_____

_____

CHANGE

My insight, awareness and responses: _____

_____

_____

_____

_____

_____

_____

_____

_____

NOTE TO SELF

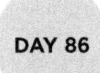

DAY 86   DAY & DATE _____

CIRCUMSTANCES

Who/Where/When: _____

_____

_____

_____

What happened? _____

_____

_____

_____

MY REACTIONS

What I felt: _____

_____

_____

What I thought: _____

_____

_____

What I did: _____

_____

_____

CHOICES

My alternatives:

CHANGE

My insight, awareness and responses:

NOTE TO SELF

DAY 87   DAY & DATE _____

CIRCUMSTANCES

Who/Where/When: _____

_____

_____

_____

What happened? _____

_____

_____

_____

MY REACTIONS

What I felt: _____

_____

_____

What I thought: _____

_____

_____

What I did: _____

_____

_____

CHOICES

My alternatives:

_____

_____

_____

_____

_____

CHANGE

My insight, awareness and responses:

_____

_____

_____

_____

_____

_____

_____

_____

_____

NOTE TO SELF

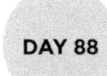 DAY & DATE _____

CIRCUMSTANCES

Who/Where/When: _____

_____

_____

_____

What happened? _____

_____

_____

_____

MY REACTIONS

What I felt: _____

_____

_____

What I thought: _____

_____

_____

What I did: _____

_____

_____

CHOICES

My alternatives:

_____

_____

_____

_____

_____

CHANGE

My insight, awareness and responses:

_____

_____

_____

_____

_____

_____

_____

_____

_____

NOTE TO SELF

DAY 89　DAY & DATE _____

CIRCUMSTANCES

Who/Where/When: _____

_____

_____

_____

What happened? _____

_____

_____

_____

MY REACTIONS

What I felt: _____

_____

_____

What I thought: _____

_____

_____

What I did: _____

_____

_____

CHOICES

My alternatives:

_____

_____

_____

_____

_____

CHANGE

My insight, awareness and responses:

_____

_____

_____

_____

_____

_____

_____

_____

NOTE TO SELF

DAY 90   DAY & DATE _____

CIRCUMSTANCES

Who/Where/When: _____

_____

_____

_____

What happened? _____

_____

_____

_____

MY REACTIONS

What I felt: _____

_____

_____

What I thought: _____

_____

_____

What I did: _____

_____

_____

CHOICES

My alternatives: _____

_____

_____

_____

_____

CHANGE

My insight, awareness and responses: _____

_____

_____

_____

_____

_____

_____

_____

_____

NOTE TO SELF

*Life can only
be understood
backwards; but
it must be lived
forwards.*

— SOREN KIERKEGAARD

LIVING FORWARDS

The writer Annie Dillard shares this wisdom with us: *How we spend our days is, of course, how we spend our lives.* Each day is an opportunity to learn something of value about how we might better spend the next one. Over the past ninety days you have given yourself the opportunity to learn from your everyday experiences. Now you have the chance to reflect on how you might use those stories to shape your life and create the future you want to see.

Use the following four pages to highlight and cross reference the moments, stories and notes to self from the past ninety days that have had the biggest impact on you. What things do you want to remember to help you to live forwards? Which of these will you take action on?

LESSONS

Things I have learned

Insight	Page
1.	
2.	
3.	
4.	
5.	
6.	
7.	
8.	
9.	
10.	

INSIGHTS

Things I now understand

Insight	Page
1.	
2.	
3.	
4.	
5.	
6.	
7.	
8.	
9.	
10.	

IDEAS

Things I want to explore

Insight	Page
1.	
2.	
3.	
4.	
5.	
6.	
7.	
8.	
9.	
10.	

PLANS

Things I want to do

Insight	Page
1.	
2.	
3.	
4.	
5.	
6.	
7.	
8.	
9.	
10.	

ACKNOWLEDGEMENTS

Just as a story unfolds, this journal has unfolded over many iterations with the help of family, friends, colleagues and The Story Skills Workshop students. First, I want to thank my dear friend and colleague, Seth Godin, for helping me to become a braver, better teacher.

Thanks to every member of The Story Skills Workshop coaching team, who show up with their whole hearts to help others find and tell their stories. My friends: Mark Dyck, Tom Huntingdon, Anne Roche, Luke Harris, Enrika Greathouse, Cat Preston, Kira Higgs, Conor McCarthy and Paula Braun, your work matters.

Thanks to my dear friend Kelly Exeter, not just for designing the journal but for always putting the reader first.

My love and thanks to my son, Matt Jiwa, who wrote the single most valuable sentence in this book. And who made me believe the idea was worth pursuing because it made sense to him, one of the wisest people I know. To his brothers Adam and Kieran, thanks for loving and cheering me on. And to my husband Moyez, my first patient reader, who walks the path with me, always.

ABOUT THE AUTHOR

Bernadette Jiwa is a bestselling author and creator of The Story Skills Workshop—the groundbreaking online program, that has helped thousands of people to unlock the magic in their stories. She grew up in Dublin, the storytelling capital of the world. Now she lives in the world's most liveable city, Melbourne, Australia. Her work takes her from Singapore to New York and everywhere in between. You can find her at thestoryoftelling.com.

Made in United States
North Haven, CT
02 March 2024

49493986R00134